# AND THEN GOD CREATED THE MIDDLE EAST AND SAID 'LET THERE BE BREAKING NEWS'

Karl

SAQI

ABDESHMUN AND HANNO:

The Phoenicians Invent Speech Bubbles

# Contents

# GEOGRAPHY
## FOR
# DUMMIES

People often ask me 'where is the Middle East?' It's the area between Egypt, Iran, Yemen, Turkey and the British Museum.

A telling Western phrase about the Middle East is 'borders were drawn without regard to ethnicity', as if that's a bad thing. I mean, if they had divided states by ethnicity, my grandmother's old neighbourhood in Baghdad would have been four different countries.

Sykes and Picot Go Out for a Pizza

You may wonder why the Middle East gets so much airtime. Well, regions of the world were competing to host the apocalypse and the Middle East won.

When God put Europe near the Middle East, it was an Occident waiting to happen.

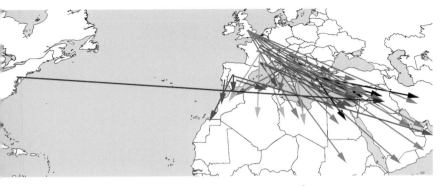

WESTERN INVASIONS OF THE MIDDLE EAST

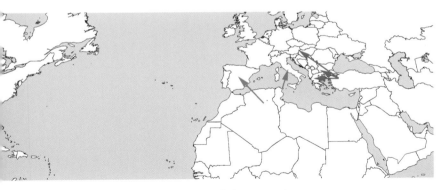

VS THE OTHER WAY ROUND

I don't know how the tradition of each new US president rearranging the Middle East like they're redecorating came about, but it's high time they found another hobby.

War is an expensive way to learn geography.

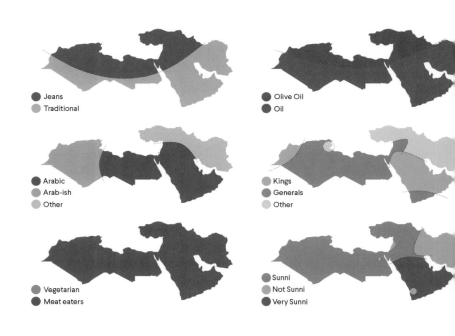

Jeans
Traditional

Olive Oil
Oil

Arabic
Arab-ish
Other

Kings
Generals
Other

Vegetarian
Meat eaters

Sunni
Not Sunni
Very Sunni

Six New Ways to Divide the Middle East and North Africa

Arabic is technically the fifth most-spoken language in the world, but if you discount the words *inshallah* and *habibi* it drops to number seventy-three.

As one of my own extra-curricular activities, I'm making the Arab version of *Homeland*. The US scenes will be filmed in Iceland and we will get Australians to play the American roles.

EXPORTS
AND
IMPORTS

The two main exports from the Middle East are oil and news.

... And now you know why they call it the Purge-*ian* Gulf.

It's based on a religion from Palestine, an alphabet from Iraq and Lebanon, and an urban model from Syria, but let's call it 'Western' civilisation.

For an Arab to be fluent in English: write a PhD.
For a Westerner to be fluent in Arabic: order lunch.

You can't take a laptop on a flight to the US, but the US is free to fly jets full of bombs into the Middle East. That's balance for you.

It seems the US exported so much democracy to the Middle East, it ran out of it.

When the Ottomans attacked Vienna, it gave Europe croissants. When the US invaded Iraq, it gave the Middle East ISIS.

They should give hurricanes names like Mohammed or Fatima. It would make it much harder for them to enter the US.

While Khalil Gibran is famous in the West for his writing, in Lebanon he is famous for getting an American visa on his first attempt.

When I travel abroad, I toss my clothes casually into a suitcase, because I know that, as an Arab, I will be searched at the airport and security will fold my shirts and trousers neatly for me.

I hate it when people stereotype you because you're an Arab. Yesterday someone asked me to introduce algebra to European languages.

As a Middle Eastern person, when you visit a museum in Europe, it feels like when you visit friends and see a book you lent them years ago proudly displayed in their bookcase.

# REPORTING
# BREAKING
# NEWS

And then God created the Middle East and said,
'Let there be breaking news and analysis'.

The main worry I have about driverless cars is how Western journalists would get their stories in the Arab world with no taxi drivers to talk to.

I like to think that there's an alternative internet where Arab taxi drivers write about their amusing encounters with foreign reporters and their simple worldview.

What is it about the Middle East that makes journalists want to describe a person's eye colour as a specific shade of coffee in a political article?

Reporter: 'I'm here in a war zone, bombs are falling around me, there's an earthquake ...'

Presenter: 'We apologise for the poor sound quality.'

We Arabs are like, 'You can't report on Arab countries without learning Arabic'.

*Learns Arabic.*

'Why do you know Arabic? You must be a spy.'

In excellent news from Lebanon, railway employees have had a pay rise. Despite the fact that there are no railways.

Lebanese headlines make even the truth sound like a lie.

So to recap, Syria's war is a civil war wrapped in a proxy war, entangled with a holy war and enmeshed with yet another holy war.

# THE
# MIDDLE EAST
# PROBLEM

My favourite thing is when pundits say: 'This aspect of the Middle East is complex, thorny and very difficult to understand. Here's my 500-word article explaining it all.'

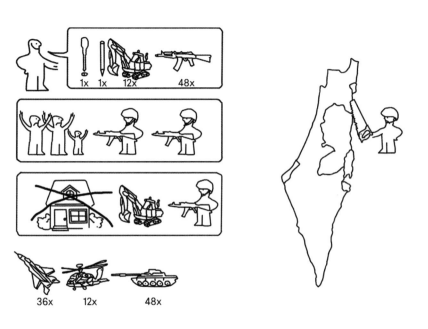

Israeli FM: Swedish Government Needs to Understand that
Relations in the Middle East are More Complicated than IKEA Furniture

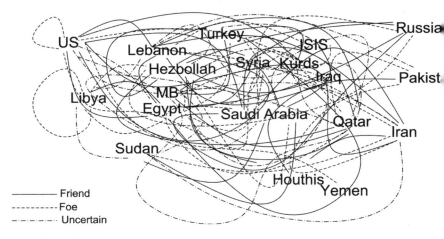

Friend
------- Foe
-----·-----·- Uncertain

Note: Palestine and Israel
have been excluded for
the sake of simplicity.

Diagram of Geopolitical Relationships in the Middle East

I'm deeply grateful to Westerners who, despite being in the midst of a historic crisis of their own, still take the time to lecture us.

BUY YOURS NOW!
(Warning: They don't do anything,
but they last a very long time.)

Lebanese Politician Inaction Figures

I would stay out of internal Saudi politics, but since they took it upon themselves to hire and fire Lebanon's prime minister, I have started treating their business as internal affairs.

Lebanese Politics: The Board Game

If you remove the US, UK, France, Russia, Iran, Saudi, Syria, Israel, Qatar, Turkey, Kuwait and Egypt, Lebanese politics is very simple.

I don't know what gives Western opinionators the impression that the Middle East is a puzzle they have to solve.

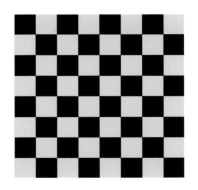

International
Chess Board

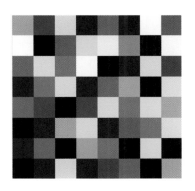

Arab
Chess Board

Arab Chess Board versus International Chess Board.
Embrace the Ambiguity.

An Arab dictator is like a matryoshka doll in reverse.
Every time you remove one, you get a bigger one.

WAR
AND
PEACE

I love how they call them 'World War' I and II. It's the Europeans' idea of being inclusive and allowing us to share the credit for their wars.

The thing I don't get about the Clash of Civilisations is how the West and Islam made it to the final.

In a surprising turn of events, the Clash of Civilisations now features a Sunni-Jewish-Protestant axis versus a Shi'i-Orthodox-Atheist axis.

People think my hatred of the West is as a result of recent foreign policy, but in truth I never got over the Sack of Constantinople.

An Ancient Arab Proverb

The enemy of my enemy is not my friend, but may be provided with aerial intelligence to support ground operations.

As an aside, North Korea will soon stop releasing missiles one by one and will launch them all together as a box set.

Saudi Arabia and Iran set an excellent example of two guys shouting at each other in a bar, but not quite ready to take it outside just yet.

We can all relate to various domestic situations in the Middle East. For example, I have learned from Saudi royal family politics how to sow discord among my children to prevent them from ganging up on me.

America's War on Terror is going very well. It has now isolated al-Qaida in the small area between Afghanistan and West Africa.

**RE**

## INTERNATIONAL AFFAIRS

**YAR**

### Seeking Moderate Opposition

The United States Government is seeking moderate Syrian opposition for its next war. Willingness to cooperate is crucial. Focus on fighting ISIS is a must, other aims unimportant. Send CV and cover letter to recruit@cia.gov or call 202-747-6800 and ask for John. Urgent. Secrecy guaranteed.

## HEALTH

## PEST CONTROL

**LAKE**

The US Strategy for Fighting ISIS

Meanwhile, Iraq seems to be invading itself for the oil.

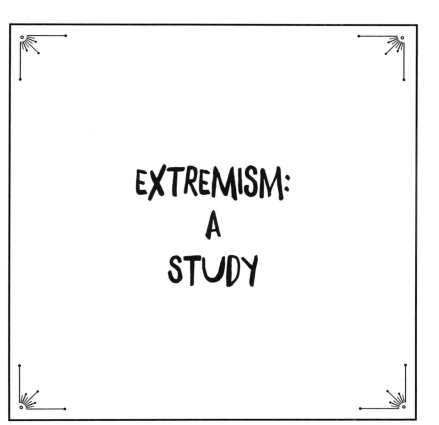

# EXTREMISM:
# A
# STUDY

You want the simple one-line explanation for what caused ISIS? Here goes:

The failure of the postcolonial elites to create genuine democratic societies and foster a sense of national unity opting instead for military dictatorships that eroded the potential for economic and political development coupled with the historic mistakes of Arab progressive parties and their appeasement towards autocratic rulers contributing to the complete evisceration of alternative political frameworks that could create organic resistance towards external meddling, hegemony and outright military interventions leaving a radical interpretation of religion as the only remaining ideological platform capable of mobilising the disenfranchised that was then exacerbated by the global decline of universal ideals and the rise of identity as a prime mobiliser and enabled by political and financial support from theocratic regimes aiming to shore up their legitimacy and made worse by the collapse of the regional security order creating the conditions for proxy wars and political, social and economic upheaval intensified by geo-politically incoherent international meddling escalating conflicts and leading to a perpetual state of chaos under which the appeal of a revivalist religious-political order embodied by the caliphate becomes attractive particularly when coupled with a millenarian apocalyptic narrative.

Simple.

You can tell that ISIS members aren't *real* Arabs because they're desperate to have the apocalypse on time. No Arab has ever been this keen on punctuality.

I personally don't think we should worry about ISIS. Launching a magazine was a fatal mistake; it will bankrupt them within years.

I love statistics like: 'bees have killed more people than ISIS'. True, but bees aren't a death cult.

I also love the ISIS belief that if a man is killed by a woman he doesn't go to heaven. Actually, you go, but you have to cook and clean for eternity.

How many ISIS jihadis does it take to change a lightbulb?

... What's wrong with eternal darkness?

'I'm the caliph', Baghdadi said.
'I will instil awe and dread.'
Then the walls came down,
He ran out of town,
And nobody knows if he's alive or dead.

I disagreed with the idea that reality has become too strange to satirise. Then I read that bin Laden was radicalised by Shakespeare.

I have decided to become a fundamentalist myself and revive a bygone Arab era. My aims are drinking, smoking and partying like 1960s Beirut and Baghdad.

Considering the instability and rise of extremism in the West, I think the West should invade itself for the sake of consistency.

# RELIGIOUS HARMONY

ABDESHMUN AND HANNO:
THE PHOENICIANS INVENT POLYTHEISM

The ancients had gods of love, war, fertility, healing, prosperity, rain and sun, truth and wisdom. We have apps for those now.

God: 'Aha, I found it. I shall launch the Abrahamic religions from here, the perfect spot. Why don't I put most of the oil here also'.

We're actually very proud of God in the Middle East. He's the local guy who went on to acquire international fame.

Early Christians in the Middle East: 'We must export our new religion to the West, it will bring us closer together'. That went well.

If a medieval time traveller appeared today and picked up a newspaper, they'd think: 'Caliphate, crusades ... nothing new then.'

If you want God to laugh, tell Him your plans for the day after a regime change in an Arab country.

THE PARTY OF GOD

THE WAR FOR GOD

There's nothing that thrills Western journalists more than discovering a 'new' ethnic or religious group in the Middle East.

The thing about Abrahamic religions is that Christianity and Islam are like cover versions of Judaism.

Twelve people just started to follow me. Jesus.

Personally, I prefer religion to science. Religion has ten clear commandments, whereas the rules of science change every day. 'Don't go out in the sun, no sugar, no egg yolks, no meat, no milk'.

You see, among Arab atheists now, it matters which God you don't believe in.

One day, atheism will be properly established in the Arab world. *Inshallah*.

Wahahahahabism: A fundamentalist Middle Eastern comedy movement.

# DEMOCRACY
# FOR
# REALISTS

Do you understand how voting works
in the Arab world? (Tick one)

Yes ☐

Yes ☐

If we ever did a Yes/No referendum in an Arab country, most people would reply *inshallah* anyway.

It took a year to start the Brexit negotiations while Saudi Arabia and sidekicks finished Qatarexit in days. That's Arab efficiency for you.

I love how political analysts talk about 'the Arabs' as a unit, as if all 400 million of us sat around the village square and decided things. We can't agree on a single falafel recipe, you think we have one view on politics?

Many people are asking me why I'm not commenting on the Arab Summit. Not into them anymore, I preferred their early work.

But while there are so many women leaders in the world today, we haven't managed to elect a single woman Arab dictator yet. So sad.

THE NEW EGYPT

The New Egypt: Monopoly

Turkey remains determined not to miss out on the fun. Erdogan will soon have to hire public servants just so he can fire them because he's surely running out of people to purge.

My favourite Erdogan quote: 'Why drink wine when you can eat the grapes?' Indeed, and why eat a kebab when you can bite the cow?

The US's anti-communist strategy worked wonders.
They got rid of poets and replaced them with jihadis.

The only real difference between political systems is that under communism you buy everything from a single state outlet, whereas under fully-mature capitalism you buy everything from Amazon.

Every time there's an election in a Western country the world holds its breath in fear. The solution is clear: stop having elections.

The only thing we know for certain about Macron is that he is 40 years old and even that will probably change next year.

2011: yay, social media can disrupt the political order.

2017: shit, social media can disrupt the political order.

Nazis, Take 1: 'We're going to dominate the world and annihilate everyone else.'

Nazis, Take 2: 'We're just a misunderstood minority.'

If Twitter were a soap opera, now would be a good time for Trump to have an accident involving an out of control home appliance.

I'm not saying you can't get a Trump in the Arab world, but it would at least require a military coup.

# DOMESTIC BLISS

The stages of Western civilisation:

1. Feudalism
2. Enlightenment
3. Industrial revolution
4. Modernity
5. Po-Mo
6. Inventing new hummous 'flavours'

The main difference between Arabs and Westerners is that the latter will queue for half an hour for a falafel wrap.

My friends in the UK always insist I go camping with them. And I'm like, dude, I'm Lebanese – no electricity, running water or internet isn't leisure for me.

Strangely, I didn't start to feel British until the country became dysfunctional.

In Arab culture if you are offered food you say no twice and yes on the third time. Much like a European referendum.

Another fun cultural fact for you: in Arabic a chicken is called *dejaja*. A chicken you ate yesterday is called *déjà-ja*.

There are many Spanish words that originate from Arabic, like *alatar* (perfume dealer), *alvarez* (knight) and *almodóvar*, which means 'cult filmmaker'.

These two facts are apparently unrelated: wine was invented in the Middle East. God has only appeared to people in the Middle East.

In the Middle East, we have four annual seasons: slumber, hope, rejuvenation and dashed expectations.

We have slightly different attitudes to the passing of time in the East and West. In the West, listening to 'oldies' means a song from the 1980s. In the Middle East, it would be a song from Andalusia from a millennium ago.

After the Arab awakening comes the Arab siesta.

# BAR JOKES

A Muslim, a Christian and a Jew walk into a bar. According to new guidelines on religious tolerance, they enjoy a mutually respectful time.

A Maronite, a Sunni, a Shi'i, a Druze, a Greek Orthodox, a Greek Catholic, An Arm—

There isn't enough space in this format for a Lebanese bar joke.

Fairouz walks into a bar. The moon caresses the olive tree.

Umm Kulthum walks into a bar. Walks into a bar. Walks into a bar. Walks into a baaaaaaaaaaaaaarrrrrrrrrrrrrrrrrrrr.

Marx, Lenin and Trotsky walk into a bar. Marx argues the punchline is inevitable. Lenin has a five-year plan. Trotsky flirts with a woman.

Later, Stalin orders Trotsky be removed from the original joke and inserts himself instead. He decrees punchlines are a bourgeois indulgence.

Žižek and Chomsky walk into a bar. Chomsky says the punchline is empirically wrong. Žižek uses a Lacanian metaphor about Chomsky's mother.

Three Iranian presidential candidates walk into a bar. We're waiting for the Supreme Leader to issue the punchline.

Three Arab commentators walk into a bar. They get funding from the EU and call it 'A Panel Discussion on the Arab Spring'.

Gaddafi, Mubarak and Ben Ali walk into a bar. After they leave, the Muslim Brotherhood win the elections, ban alcohol and close the bar.

So Putin and Erdogan walk into a bar. Sorry, a war.

Three Arab post-colonialists walk into a bar. They refuse to continue the joke because it's based on White Man stereotypes.

Three conspiracy theorists walk into a bar. Do you think it's a coincidence?

Three EU commissioners walk into a bar. The punchline is utterly incomprehensible but available in twenty-four languages.

A minimalist walks into a bar.

# Karl reMarks

Karl reMarks is a Middle East political and cultural online commentary, with frequent forays into satire. It is written by Karl Sharro, whose work has been featured in the *Guardian*, *Wall Street Journal*, *Economist*, BBC, Ted-X Talks and Al Jazeera, among others. In 2016, Karl's video, 'The Simple One-Sentence Explanation for What Caused Isis,' went viral, with 1.6 million views on Facebook alone. Alongside his role as a satirist and commentator on the Middle East, Karl has practised architecture in London and Beirut. His avatar is taken from his cartoon series 'The Phoenicians Invented Everything.'

www.karlremarks.com
@KarlreMarks

Published 2018 by Saqi Books

Book design by Will Brady.

ISBN 978 0 86356 902 9
eISBN 978 0 86356 907 4

A full CIP record for this book is available from the British Library.

Printed by PBtisk a.s.

Saqi Books
26 Westbourne Grove
London W2 5RH
www.saqibooks.com